Y PAPERS

Thomas Cranmer and the English Reformation

by

David Loades

HEADSTART HISTORY

Published by   HEADSTART HISTORY
                    PO Box 41, Bangor, Gwynedd, LL57 1SB

Set by   C.B.S.
                    155 Hamilton Road,
                    Felixstowe, Suffolk, IP11 7DR

Printed by   THE IPSWICH BOOK COMPANY LTD
                    The Drift, Nacton Road,
                    Ipswich, Suffolk IP3 3QR

ISBN   1 873041 40 3

A CIP catalogue record for this book is available from the
British Library.

CONTENTS

Introduction

Frontispiece :   Thomas Cranmer by Gerlach Flicke

By kind permission of the National
Portrait Gallery

INTRODUCTION

The HEADSTART HISTORY PAPERS aim to identify themes and topics the significance of which extends beyond the studies of professional historians. The PAPERS are distillations of the research of distinguished historians in a form appropriate to students and to the general reader.

The life and work of Thomas Cranmer spanned one of the most important periods in English history. He was consecrated Archbishop of Canterbury at a time when Henry VIII was being thwarted by the papacy in his wish to end his marriage to Catherine of Aragon and when the authority of the Roman Catholic Church in England was being challenged. The King's Great Matter and the desire for reform had a profound effect on the future of both church and state. The legislation masterminded by Thomas Cromwell ended the role of the papacy in England and Wales and established the Anglican church with the king as Supreme Head. The Church in England had always been distinctive within the context of Western Christendom but after the break with Rome it developed a distinctive liturgy through the work of Thomas Cranmer. The high point of this achievement was the Second Prayer Book of 1552 a work still admired for the beauty of its language and elegant style points noted by the Prince of Wales in 1989, the 500th anniversary of the birth of Cranmer.

Cranmer was the first Protestant Archbishop of Canterbury. His martyrdom was a tragedy during Mary's short reign when the Roman Church struggled through its brief restoration. Cranmer might have been remembered for no more than his painful recantation but as David Loades points out, his memorial was assured when Elizabeth I succeeded her sister Mary to the throne of England and restored the Church which the Archbishop had led. Thus

'Thomas Cranmer stands at the head of a liturgical and ecclesiastical tradition which not only lives on in this country but has followed the Imperial flag and commercial enterprise of Britain into all the corners of the world.'

David Loades' early research was supervised by Geoffrey Elton and this work led to *Two Tudor Conspiracies* and *The Oxford Martyrs*. The latter reflected his early interest in Cranmer and led to his distinguished work on both the life and reign of Mary Tudor which established him as one of Britain's leading Tudor historians. He has continued his research on Mary, published a book on the Tudor Court and has recently completed a major work on the Tudor navy as well as shorter works on the mid-Tudor crisis and the English Reformation. The immense scholarship of David Loades is reflected in his numerous articles and books and the editing of important collections of articles notably for the Ecclesiastical History Society of which he is President in 1992.

HEADSTART HISTORY is fortunate in its authors but in this instance the author is captive to publishing pressure and I must thank my husband for his contribution to my success. His work on the Tudor Navy and the Tudor Court both have medieval origins which have been recorded in MEDIEVAL HISTORY the journal launched by HEADSTART HISTORY in January 1991. But David has always been on hand for advice and practical assistance. I record with pleasure my gratitude for his help and couple with that my thanks to a distinguished author for joining a distinguished series.

Judith Loades
Bangor, 1991

Thomas Cranmer

Thomas Cranmer was the first protestant archbishop of Canterbury. He was consecrated on 30 March 1533, having been duly provided to the see by Pope Clement VII, and burned at the stake in Oxford on the 21 March 1556, having been duly condemned for heresy by Pope Paul IV. His dramatic career would have been of interest only to professional historians, had it not been for the fact that two-and-a-half years after his death the Crown of England passed by inheritance to Elizabeth, and that she restored to power the protestant church which he had led, thus making him a founding father and martyr of an establishment which was to endure to the present day. Because of this quirk of fate - or act of Divine Providence - Thomas Cranmer stands at the head of a liturgical and ecclesiastical tradition which not only lives on in this country, but has followed the Imperial flag and commercial enterprise of Britain into all the corners of the world. Now that the tide of Empire has ebbed, the bishops of the Anglican communion assembling at Lambeth constitute one of the few positive reminders of the contribution which this country has made to the process of civilisation.

Thomas Cranmer was an important man, not because he was a saint, or a great theologian (he was neither of those things), but because he was able to take the unique ecclesiastical polity devised in England between 1530 and 1540, to develop it, and to make it work. The model which he thus created was particularly suited, both to the needs of the Tudor monarchy and to the instinct of emerging national self consciousness. It was for those reasons that the shrewd and pragmatic Elizabeth reimposed it, and her longevity and success guaranteed its future security. Before 1529, however, it would have been hard to forecast such a destiny for a man who seems to have deliberately courted obscurity. Cranmer was born in July 1489, the second son of a minor Nottinghamshire gentleman.[1] His early upbringing was that which was then deemed to be appropriate to his status, and owed more to the stables and the kennels than it did to the school which he attended. But his father died in 1501, and two years later his mother entered him at Jesus College, Cambridge. This was not a normal course for a young gentleman, as it would have been a hundred years later, and since he seems to have displayed no exceptional academic talent it must be presumed that his position in the family had indicated a career in the church. If so, the investment was slow to mature. For eight years he followed the traditional arts curriculum, 'nosseled in the grossest kind of sophistry . . . chiefly in the dark riddles and quidities of Duns (Scotus) and other subtle questionists', as one of his earliest biographers was to put it.[2] In 1511, at the mature age of twenty two, he graduated without distinction. Perhaps he was a late developer who was beginning at last to show aptitude, or perhaps he just lacked the initiative to do anything else, but in spite of his poor showing Cranmer stayed on at Jesus,

---

1 'Thomas Cranmer, the son of Thomas Cranmer of Aslocton esquire, and of Agnes Hatfield his wife, daughter of Laurence Hatfield of Willoughby, of like degree . . .' J.G. Nichols, *Narratives of the days of the Reformation* (Camden Society, 1859), 218.

2 *Ibid.*, 219

and proceeded to his M.A. in July 1514. By that time, his studies had begun to take a significant and new direction. Humanist influence had been gaining ground at Cambridge for a decade although, as is usual in such situations, it had made no impression upon the formal curriculum. Cranmer began to familiarise himself with the works of Erasmus and Faber, became a good classical latinist, and commenced the study of Greek and Hebrew. At about the time of his second graduation he was elected to a fellowship, and his career seemed to be moving slowly along conventional lines.

In 1516, however, at the age of 27, he resigned his fellowship in order to marry. This episode has loomed large in the folklore of the English reformation, but in truth little is known about it. Contrary to what was later reported, his wife seems to have been of suitable status, but she died less than a year later, taking their child to the grave with her.[3] Jesus College then took the unprecedented step of re-electing Cranmer to his fellowship. By 1520 he had been ordained priest, and in 1521 he proceeded Bachelor of Divinity. His marriage had proved a brief interlude, but a significant one. Like Thomas More, he seems to have felt that he lacked the gift of chastity, and preferred an honest solution to the conventional one adopted (among others) by Wolsey. Also, his college clearly recognised an exceptional talent, and one which had, as yet, made no mark upon the outside world. In

---

3 Her name was Joan, and it was later claimed that she was a barmaid at the 'Dolphin' Inn in Cambridge, an accusation which seems to have arisen from the fact that they lived there during their brief marriage. Jasper Ridley, *Thomas Cranmer*, 16-7.

1525 he became Reader in Divinity, having turned down the chance to become a founding fellow of Cardinal College, Oxford, and in 1526 he disputed successfully for his doctorate of Divinity. By this time he was recognised as a man of the 'new learning', a follower of Erasmus and John Colet and an earnest biblical scholar. As an examiner in Divinity he had a fierce reputation for failing candidates whom he judged to be insufficiently learned in the scriptures. This placed him firmly among the reforming party in the university, and aroused the fury of academic conservatives, but he had the full support of the authorities, and was not thought to be in any sense unorthodox. He was willing to read Lutheran books, but had no connection with the suspect 'White Horse' group, nor with any of the individual Cambridge radicals of the period, such as Bilney, Frith or Barnes.[4] The remarkable thing about Thomas Cranmer in 1529, when he reached the age of 40, was that, in spite of an excellent reputation for learning, he had written nothing, held no benefice, and had exercised no administrative office more responsible than that of proctors' auditor.

II

The political and religious situation into which Cranmer was to be catapulted by the events of that year is a familiar one to all students of the period. Henry VIII had been trying for about two years to repudiate his marriage to Catherine of Aragon, and had been repeatedly frustrated by the political power of the Emperor

---

4 W.A. Clebsch, *England's Earliest Protestants*, 42-54, 99-112. A.G. Dickens, *The English Reformation*, 75-83.

Charles V (Catherine's nephew) over the Pope. Also, for about a decade, the influx of Lutheran books and ideas from Germany had been re-invigorating and reshaping the indigenous Lollard tradition of religious dissent. This movement was strongly scriptural and anti-papal. In 1526 William Tyndale had published, and imported into England, a translation of the New Testament; and two years later had issued an extremely radical tract entitled *The obedience of a Christian Man*,[5] in which he had argued that the Papal authority was usurped, and that authority over particular churches belonged to the secular rulers of the countries concerned. It is too early to speak of 'English protestants' in 1529 - the term itself was not invented until 1530 - but there were certainly a number of people, particularly in the universities, at court, and in the mercantile community of London, who had absorbed an unco-ordinated mixture of heretical ideas. The bishops were worried, and steps were being taken to increase control over printed books. What made the situation particularly delicate was the fact that so many of these radical ideas were obviously useful for the king's purposes; and although Henry had never shown any sympathy with doctrinal heresy, his attitude towards the papacy had become understandably ambivalent. When Cardinal Campeggio adjourned his Legatine court on 31 July, the king desperately needed a new initiative, and the man who appeared to provide it was Thomas Cranmer.

This unlikely situation came about because there was

---

5 The 1526 *New Testament* was printed in Antwerp by Van Ruremund, and the 1528 *Obedience of a Christian man and how Christian rulers ought to governe* also in Antwerp by J. Hoochstraten. It was claimed that Anne Boleyn brought the latter work to Henry's attention.

plague in Cambridge, and Cranmer took refuge with the family of two of his pupils at Waltham in Essex. While he was there, Henry visited a minor residence which he had nearby, and as was normal in such cases, boarded out a number of his servants and courtiers with neighbouring gentry. It thus came about that Cranmer found himself at dinner with two old Cambridge acquaintances, Edward Foxe and Stephen Gardiner, both rising in royal service, and willing to listen to any ideas which would promote their master's interests and their own careers. Exactly what transpired we do not know, but Cranmer seems to have argued that the issue was one of theology rather than canon law, and could only be resolved by scriptural authority. Since Henry had already convinced himself that his case rested upon a text of Leviticus,[6] this was no more than a hopeful beginning. What the king really needed was some means whereby to elevate an Old Testament prohibition above all ecclesiastical authority, including that of the Pope. Such a theory lay ready to hand in the Lutheran doctrine of *sola scriptura*, and if its heretical antecedents could be disguised by a skilled and sympathetic theologian, then perhaps it could be called into service. This was the opportunity which Foxe and Gardiner seem to have spotted in Cranmer's discourse. When he returned to Cambridge, it was with instructions to research the possibilities, and he quickly became an enthusiastic advocate of the king's cause.

---

6 'If a man takes his brother's wife, it is an impurity; he has uncovered his brother's nakedness, they shall be childless'. Leviticus 20: 21. Ralph Wakefield, the humanist scholar also seems to have persuaded the king that, in the original Hebrew, the text read '. . . they shall be without sons'; *The Divorce Tracts of Henry VIII*, ed. E. Surtz and V. Murphy, xiii.

This made him distinctly unpopular with his colleagues, and probably indicates that he had already abandoned the orthodox position on Papal sovereignty. By October reports of his success had reached the court, and he was summoned to see Henry at Greenwich. When he left it was with a commission to write a learned treatise justifying the king's position, and instructions to reside with the Earl of Wiltshire at Durham House while he did so.[7] His Cambridge days were over, and his public career about to commence.

The work which Cranmer wrote during the last two months of 1529 does not survive, but we know that Henry was very pleased with it, and sent its author to Rome as a special envoy at the end of January 1530. There he resided from April to September in a futile attempt to persuade Clement VII to allow a public disputation of the king's cause. What he did obtain, and in the circumstances it was a remarkable achievement for an embryo diplomat, was a number of favourable judgements, or *censurae*, from Italian universities, and permission from the Pope for these judgements to be issued.[8] Perhaps Henry was disappointed, for no immediate reward followed these efforts, and for the next two years it was the Boleyns rather than the king who patronised Cranmer and provided him with the context in which to develop his ideas. It was not until the end of 1531 that he

---

7 Thomas Boleyn, Earl of Wiltshire, was Anne Boleyn's father.

8 Contrary to traditional accounts, it was not Cranmer's idea to collect these *censurae*, but as an experienced academic he was an obvious agent to use. Guy Bedouelle and Patrick Le Gal, *Le 'Divorce' du Roi Henry VIII; etudes et documents*, 49-57.

formally entered royal service as a chaplain, and was given his first ecclesiastical preferment, the Archdeaconry of Taunton. Henry had already told the Emperor that he had found a new theological champion, and he now gave his adversary the chance to inspect his champion by sending Cranmer to him as a resident ambassador. The nine months which he then spent tracking Charles around his vast dominions were the most momentous and adventurous of his life. He saw secular politics for the first time at the highest level, and encountered the Lutheran theologians on their own ground. After a fruitless mission he was summoned home in December 1532, having acquired a whole variety of new perspectives on Henry, upon his problems, and upon the life of the church. In spite of what was later alleged, he had not been converted to Lutheranism, and there is no evidence that he ever accepted the confession of Augsburg, but he had certainly gained a fresh insight into the value of vernacular scripture, and also into the liturgical possibilities of translation. It was the worship rather than the doctrine of the Evangelical churches which impressed him. He had also acquired a second wife. His first marriage was an obscure episode, but it had at least been a lawful choice. This was quite different. In 1532 Cranmer was an ordained priest, on a public mission from his sovereign, and with every prospect of a successful career in the church. Why he chose to marry Margaret, the niece of the Lutheran Divine Andreas Osiander, remains a mystery. The couple did not speak each other's languages, and can have known each other only for a matter of weeks. Moreover, no matter what the future held for him in England, public acknowledgement of his marriage would be unthinkable for the foreseeable future. In the event their relationship was to remain clandestine for fifteen years, and Margaret must have been an incredibly long-suffering woman; but she appears to have been devoted to her husband, and married twice more after his death.

It is not surprising, in these circumstances, that Cranmer found the summons home unwelcome, and the reason for the summons made the whole situation infinitely worse. William Warham, the Archbishop of Canterbury, had died in August 1532, and the king decided, at last, to make a decisive move. Some of his advisers, particularly Edward Foxe, Nicholas de Burgo, and more recently Thomas Cromwell, had been urging him to seek a solution to his problem in England.[9] Anne Boleyn's frustration was only matched by Henry's own, and the vacancy at Canterbury presented a unique opportunity. The Archdeacon of Taunton was by no means an obvious person to promote to the metropolitan see, but he had one special qualification. On the issue which really mattered at that moment, he was whole-heartedly and honestly the king's man. The news undoubtedly took Cranmer by surprise (as well it might), and his professions of unworthiness had a more than conventional vehemence. It was one thing for a clerical diplomat to evade the law of celibacy, and to flirt with heretical liturgies, it was a different matter for the Archbishop of Canterbury to do the same. Nevertheless, there was no escape, except by running away and hiding in Germany; ' . . . there was

9 Graham Nicholson, 'The Act of Appeals and the English Reformation', in C. Cross, D. Loades and J. Scarisbrick, *Law and Government under the Tudors*, 19-30.

never man came more unwillingly to a bishopric than I did to that' he later declared. Nevertheless, by the middle of January 1533 he was back in London, and his appointment was made public. Within a few days of his arrival Anne Boleyn was discovered to be pregnant, and on 26 January the king secretly married her. The archbishop-elect did not know about this until later, but he did not need to. He realised that as soon as he was consecrated he would be expected to annul Henry's first marriage. In itself that presented no problem to his conscience, but consecration involved an oath of obedience to the papacy which he would immediately be forced to break. Somewhat surprisingly Clement, who knew Cranmer's views, issued the Bulls without protest, and it was left to the Archbishop himself to prefix his oath with a formal protestation that it would not bind his conscience against the laws of God, or the realm of England. On 28 May, just three days before Anne's scheduled coronation, and after a show of due process, he formally declared that Catherine of Aragon was not, and never had been, Henry's wife.

III

Cranmer was thus committed to the Royal Supremacy before any such theory had been formulated, let alone applied. He was obviously an instrument of the king's will, but there is no evidence that he did violence to his own conscience in the process, because he believed that the monarch's authority derived from God, and was answerable only to heaven. As archbishop, he might be called upon to advise Henry over issues of conscience, just as a secular councillor might be called upon to advise over issues of policy, but the decision was the king's, and was not to be questioned. Consequently in 1536 he annulled the Boleyn marriage on the grounds of an impediment which had existed, and which he knew to have existed, when he had pronounced the marriage good in 1533.[10] It was not a straightforward matter, and the king's conscience had conveniently shifted. Understandably he was accused, both at the time and later, of being a mere time server; but the accusation was not justified. Like Stephen Gardiner, he was the king's man, and it was only after Henry's death that he began to discover alternative principles of allegiance. The king knew this perfectly well, and there was a precious honesty about Cranmer's commitment which retained Henry's confidence throughout the vicissitudes of the latter part of the reign.

> 'I would you should well understand', he told
> a hostile council in 1543, 'that I account my
> Lord of Canterbury as faithful a man towards
> me as ever was prelate in this realm, and one
> to whom I am in many ways beholden, by the
> faith I owe unto God . . .'[11]

He was a reformer, but only within the parameters which

---

10 This was the 'affinity' created between Henry and Anne by Henry's liaison with Anne's sister, Mary. In canon law this created an impediment equivalent to marriage. Henry's second marriage could not have been annulled (as distinct from dissolved) by alleged adultery which had taken place subsequent to its celebration.

11 Nichols, *Narratives*, 258. This anecdote comes from a biography written after the archbishop's death by his secretary, Ralph Morris.

the king laid down. The publication of the Great Bible in 1538, the simplification of the calendar, and the dissolution of the monasteries between 1536 and 1540, were all policies of which he was an active promoter. But they were not his policies, and the chief executive was Thomas Cromwell. On the one theological issue which mattered profoundly to the king in the later years of his life, the doctrine of the mass, Cranmer was at this time entirely orthodox. Consequently, in spite of his secret marriage (which Henry knew about by 1540), and his patronage of radical preachers, he was able to disagree with the king, and to give him unpalatable advice, in a manner which even Thomas Cromwell envied. 'Aha, my chaplain', Henry is alleged to have told him at the time of the Prebendaries' plot in Canterbury, 'now I know who is the greatest heretic in Kent', but he completed the joke by giving Cranmer himself the commission to investigate the charges.

He was never far from controversy, and the Act of Six Articles in 1539, followed by Cromwell's fall in 1540, demonstrated that there could be a much more conservative interpretation of the Royal Supremacy, which was equally acceptable to the king. For a time, he appeared to be in serious danger; but Stephen Gardiner, his principal rival, retained a firm belief in priestly authority, which was a hostage to fortune in the 1540s. Alone among the leading prelates of the realm, Cranmer reserved no function from the secular magistrate;

> '. . . there is no certain rule prescribed or limited by the word of God for the nomination, election, presentation or appointing of

any such ecclesiastical ministers, but the same is wholly left unto the positive laws and ordinances of every Christian region, provided and made or to be made in that behalf, with the assent of the prince and ruler...'[12]

This meant that the English church was governed by bishops and ecclesiastical courts in the traditional manner, not out of obedience to the canon law, or the scriptures, but because the king had so decided. It is not surprising that Henry found such convictions irresistible, and the conservative reaction petered out by 1542. A similar attitude to the question of orders made Cranmer far more radical than Luther, or any other magisterial reformer. In a private memorandum to the king, written about 1538, he declared;

'A bishop may make a priest by the scriptures, and so may princes, and governors also, and that by the authority of God committed to them, and the people also by their election; for as we read that bishops have done it, so Christian emperors and princes usually have done it; and the people before Christian princes were, commonly did elect their bishops and priests'.[13]

---

12 *A necessary doctrine and erudition for a Christen man* (better known as *The King's Book*) of 1543, in *Formularies of the Faith put forth by authority in the reign of Henry VIII*, ed. C. Lloyd (Oxford, 1825), 278.

13 *The Works of Thomas Cranmer*, ed. J.E. Cox (Parker Society, 1846), 117.

Consecration in the traditional sense was not therefore necessary for the lawful exercise of episcopal or priestly functions, but only due appointment by a properly constituted authority. When Henry VIII died in 1547, Cranmer logically concluded that his own commission, and those of his fellow bishops, had terminated in the same manner as the tenure of any other public office in the king's gift. In February 1547 he applied to Edward VI's council for a fresh commission, to the alarm and outrage of Gardiner, who protested that he was an ordinary, not a delegate; in other words his episcopal authority derived from his consecration, and not from the king.

Cranmer had retained the old king's confidence to the end, and was a member of that group of reforming councillors who took over the government of the new reign. Henry's position had remained ambivalent to the last. The first Act for the dissolution of chantries in 1545, and the provisions which he made for the education of his son, suggest that he had swung decisively into the reforming camp at the end of his life; but his will, with its massive provision for requiem masses, points in the opposite direction. Henry had neither died nor lived a protestant, and from the catholic point of view his church had been schismatic, not heretical. However, within a few weeks of his death the situation began to change, and in the summer of 1547 Cranmer issued a Homily (or Instruction) on the central doctrine of Justification, which shows that he had by then adopted the protestant position *sola fide*.[14] The first parliament of Edward's reign,

14 Justification 'by faith alone', as opposed to the catholic position of justification (salvation) by faith and good works. These homilies were probably written earlier, and it is not clear at what point

December 1547, repealed the Act of Six Articles, and at long last allowed Margaret Cranmer to emerge from the shadows by legalising the marriage of clergy. Gardiner fought a determined rearguard action against all these changes, but his position was an illogical one as long as he continued to recognise the Royal Supremacy, and could rest upon nothing more solid than the alleged unwisdom of making major innovations during the king's minority. For Cranmer, there was no such problem. According to his own testimony it was in 1548 that he finally completed his conversion to protestantism by abandoning the traditional doctrine of transubstantiation. The position which he had then reached was distinctively his own, based upon the study of the Greek and Latin fathers, as well as upon the scriptures and contemporary continental theologians. It had taken him almost thirty years to arrive at these conclusions, and he had done so piecemeal, starting with clerical celibacy and the papal authority. After 1547 the Royal Supremacy steadily moved the English church in the direction which he approved (and largely under his guidance), so there was no tension in his allegiance. He had already prepared an English Litany in 1545, and in 1548-9 he directed, and largely wrote, that elegant translation of the Sarum Use which became the first Book of Common Prayer.

Cranmer was also keenly aware that the developments which he was promoting in England had an international significance. Luther had died in March 1546, and there was no heir to his unique authority as the founding father of the reformation. Moreover within a year the

Cranmer began to move in a protestant direction on this central issue. D. Loades, *The Oxford Martyrs*, 53.

Schmalkaldic League, the political organisation of the Lutheran princes and cities, had suffered a disastrous military defeat at the hands of the Emperor. Cranmer was convinced by the summer of 1547 that the reformation in Germany was about to be destroyed, and saw the emerging protestant church in England as the natural heir to Luther's mantle of leadership. In fact the Interim which Charles V imposed in 1548 fell a long way short of a total catholic victory, and some protestant states, such as Brandenburg, which had never been members of the Schmalkaldic League, were unaffected by its defeat. Nevertheless, where his arm was strong enough the Emperor acted to suppress the reformed churches, and that included the city of Strasbourg. Consequently, when Cranmer began to invite leading protestant divines to come to England and assist in his mission of construction, he received a more positive response that might otherwise have been the case. After some hesitation Philip Melanchthon declined. He had been Luther's closest confidant, but he was not a natural leader and his position was already being questioned. He was attracted by the possibilities in England, but seems to have felt that he could not afford to leave his beleaguered colleagues in Germany. The Italians Peter Martyr Vermigli and Bernadino Ochino, on the other hand, were in England before the end of 1547, and spent many months as the archbishop's guests before Martyr became Regius professor of Divinity at Oxford and Ochino was given a prebendal stall in Canterbury cathedral.[15] Early in 1549 they were joined by Martin Bucer and Paul Fagius, who had by then abandoned the struggle in Strasbourg. They

---

15 W.K. Jordan, *Edward VI; the young king*, 191-2.

also spent some time with Cranmer, and were presented to the king, before Bucer moved off to Cambridge, to take up the Regius chair of Divinity there. Bucer and Martyr certainly, and other guests probably, influenced the archbishop's thinking, particularly on the theology of the eucharist, where his recent conversion was still seeking a settled form of expression. None of them were particularly happy with the liturgy which he brought to parliament in January 1549, but they could see what he was trying to do, and took the imperfections in good part. 'Many puerilities are suffered to remain', wrote Francis Dryander to Bullinger in March 1549, 'lest the people should be offended by too great an innovation'.[16] The 1549 Prayer Book probably represented what Cranmer thought he could get away with in the political circumstances, rather than what he really wanted to do, and was consequently always intended to be transitional. When Stephen Gardiner announced that his conscience would allow him to use the new order, the archbishop knew that it would have to be changed sooner rather than later.

III

The Edwardian Church

The Act of Uniformity of 1549 nevertheless marked the formal conversion of the English church to a protestant base. In spite of Cranmer's serious attention to contemporary developments, it was not Lutheran, or Zwinglian,

---

16 *Original Letters relative to the English Reformation*, ed. Hastings Robinson, I, 350.

but *sui generis*, and its main distinguishing feature continued to be the royal supremacy. It was the church by law established, and it owed its form entirely to the legislative will of the king in parliament. The circumstances of the royal minority had shifted the emphasis of authority from the personal to the institutional office of the monarch, and gone a considerable way towards converting the church into a department of state for ecclesiastical affairs. At first Cranmer seems to have been perfectly happy with this change, and to have exerted himself to bring it about, but his continental friends were less enthusiastic. The church might properly be governed by a Godly Prince, but the doctrine of that church was a matter to be determined by its ministers, guided by the Holy Scripture. The problem with the English situation was that it involved 'tarrying for the magistrate', and the magistrate was neither as positive nor as zealous as he should have been. In May 1550 Martin Bucer complained that the state of religion in England was very feeble, precisely because it depended so heavily upon government action, and that action had so far been largely negative '. . . ordinances which the majority obey very grudgingly'.[17] The young king was Godly 'to a marvel', but most of his councillors were more interested in pulling down the old church than in building the new. The archbishop was not discouraged by this criticism. He was what would later be known as an Erastian, and he was keenly aware of the need to proceed with caution. During the summer of 1549, while the introduction of the Prayer Book was still causing riots and protests, he was working on a new reformed Ordinal

---

17 Bucer to Brentius, 15 May, 1550; *Original Letters*, II. 542.

in consultation with Bucer, whose *De ordinatione legitima* had exercised considerable influence over him. When he presented it to the council early in 1550, it was predictably greeted with abuse from both sides. This was a measure of the problem which the archbishop had to face, and why, in the last analysis, he had to rely on convincing the secular authorities.

He did not justify this, even to himself, on the grounds that the king was infallible, but rather by a generous definition of *adiaphora*, or 'things indifferent'. This concept had a long history in Christian irenicism, and had been recently revived and developed by Philip Melanchthon in Germany in an attempt to prevent his fellow-reformers from becoming incurably divided over forms of worship and church government. Such matters, including clerical dress, clerical celibacy, and even the existence or otherwise of religious orders, could all be classed as *adiaphora* on the grounds that they lacked any clear scriptural prescription. Once the authority of the pope and catholic tradition had been repudiated, and the ultimate authority of the bible acknowledged, such matters could, and should, be left to the discretion of Christian magistrates, even if they did not move with the speed which might be hoped for. Cranmer consequently remained unmoved, both by the radical agitations of John Hooper and John Knox, and by the opinion of Bucer that the wrath of God '. . . will very shortly blaze forth' against England if the process of reform was not implemented more fully and speedily.[18] In spite of controversy, the Ordinal was accepted, and Hooper was at length

18 *Ibid.*

constrained to accept consecration to the see of Gloucester wearing the prescribed vestments. In November
1550 the council and the bishops together launched a
campaign to remove stone altars from the parish churches,
and to replace them with wooden communion tables. At
the same time a complete revision of the Prayer Book
was also undertaken. This had probably been begun at
the same time as the revision of the Ordinal, and Cranmer
had certainly consulted both Bucer and Martyr by January 1551 when the work was formally authorised. Bucer
wrote down his advice in the form of the *Censura*, and
his influence has always been thought to have been para-
mount, but recent research suggests that Martyr may
have been equally important, and that a wide range of
advisers, both English and continental, were consulted.
The result was the fully reformed liturgy which was
approved by parliament in the second Act of Uniformity
of January 1552. The eucharistic wording was now un-
equivocally protestant, in the receptionist mode.[19] Prayers
for the dead, and all reference to vestments, had alike
disappeared. Not even the most ingenious conservative
could regard the second Book of Common Prayer as an
acceptable variant of the traditional liturgy.

The Second Act of Uniformity marked the highest point
of Cranmer's political influence. In spite of the other
influences which were undoubtedly present the prayer
book was his work, and expressed principally the theological position which he himself had reached. Thereafter he found the situation increasingly escaping from his

---

19 'Take and eat this in remembrance that Christ died for thee, and
feed on him in thy heart by faith, with thanksgiving'. *The Two
Liturgies . . . (of) the reign of Edward VI*, ed. Joseph Kelley, 279.

control. One indication of this was the insistence of the Council, on the prompting of Hooper and Knox, that a rubric be inserted in the already authorised text of the communion service, explaining that the practice of kneeling for the reception did not imply idolatry. Cranmer was opposed to this insertion, but was over ruled. More serious was the growing pressure for a doctrinal formulation, along the lines of the Augsburg confession. Cranmer was not enthusiastic, partly because any confession was bound to be controversial and potentially divisive, but partly also because it would tie the hands of the Supreme Head in a manner which he feared might be incompatible with the nature of that office - rather like a written constitution. Nevertheless, as individual bishops began to devise their own formularies to test the orthodoxy of candidates for ordination, the council in 1551 instructed the archbishop to draw up a set of articles for authorisation. This he did in consultation with Nicholas Ridley, the bishop of London, and circulated the result to the remaining bishops in draft at the beginning of 1552. In May he was peremptorily ordered to hand over the text for examination, and the council returned it to him in September, with instructions to revise certain parts.[20] By this time Cranmer was becoming thoroughly disillusioned with the dominant role which the council was assuming, a situation for which he was himself largely responsible. In his eyes the bishops were the proper agents of the king's ecclesiastical authority, but their position, including his own, was being steadily eroded. However, as long as the king was a minor, the logic of conciliar control was unavoidable, and he confined his protests to private letters. On the 24 November 1552 he

---

20 *Acts of the Privy Council* ed. J. Dasent, IV, 33.

submitted the final version of the Forty Two Articles, with a covering letter expressing the hope that they would establish 'concord and quietness' in religion for many years.[21] Having harried him into producing them the council, pre-occupied with many problems, then did nothing with them. They were not submitted to parliament in March 1553, nor to the convocation which accompanied it. Finally, on the 9 June, less than a month before the king's death, they were promulgated ostensibly upon the authority of the bishops and other 'learned and Godly men', but in reality by mere executive fiat. This time Cranmer protested openly and strongly, but was ignored.

Two other issues also contributed to the estrangement between the archbishop and the Duke of Northumberland, financial pressure upon the church and the reform of the canon law. When John Dudley, then Earl of Warwick, had sought Cranmer's alliance after helping to bring down Protector Somerset in October 1549, the arrangement had suited them both. Warwick gained Cranmer's invaluable personal influence with the king, and the archbishop secured the continuation of his programme of reform. However, Cranmer did not appreciate the diversion of so much former chantry property into private secular hands,[22] nor the attempt to strip many bishops of their revenues on the grounds of 'unlording'

---

21 Thomas Cranmer, *Miscellaneous writings and Letters*, 441

22 D. Loades, *The Oxford Martyrs*, 91-100. According to Morris, Cranmer had earlier reproved Henry VIII for diverting too much of the monastic resources in the same way, which should have been '...bestowed upon hospitals, bringing up of youth in virtue and good learning, and other things profitable for the commonwealth.' Nichols, 224.

them and returning them to their proper pastoral functions. His former unhappiness was shared by the protestant radicals, but not the latter, who consequently gained
in favour with the council. By 1552 Northumberland
was speaking of the Scottish radical John Knox as a
stimulant to the archbishop's flagging zeal. The clearest
indication of the nature of their disagreement, however,
came over Cranmer's cherished scheme for a reformed
code of Canon Law. The royal supremacy had made
nonsense of the old law, but it had continued in use for
want of a better. In 1552 the archbishop submitted a
revised scheme, which had cost him much thought and
effort. It was vehemently denounced by the common
lawyers, and by Northumberland himself, on the grounds
that it gave the bishops too much authority. With the
dissolution of parliament in March 1553 Cranmer's commission to prepare the scheme expired, and the whole
project collapsed, to his great chagrin. The royal supremacy was consequently showing an unacceptable face,
even to Cranmer, when Northumberland made his bid to
secure a protestant succession in July 1553. It was partly
for this reason that the archbishop gave no more than a
formal endorsement to the king's device, and shared with
other leading reformers, such as John Hooper, the view
that the young king's illness and death were a judgement
of God upon the English. They had failed to grasp their
evangelical opportunities, and allowed themselves to be
dominated by the 'carnal gospellers'. 'Our king is taken
from us by reason of our sins' wrote Hooper from prison
in the autumn of 1553 and Cranmer, also in prison by
that date, concurred.[23]

---

23 Hooper to Bullinger, 3 September 1553; *Original Letters*, I, 100.

V

Confession and recantation

Mary presented him with the same kind of problem which Edward had earlier presented to Stephen Gardiner. Gardiner, although a strong conservative, had shared both Cranmer's enthusiasm for the royal supremacy and his broad view of *adiaphora*, but he was stopped in his tracks by Cranmer's homily on Justification, published in July 1547. Justification by faith alone was not only heresy in his eyes, it was also contrary to the Act of Six Articles of 1539, which was still the authoritative statement of English orthodoxy. When the Act of Six Articles was repealed, the homily remained heretical. The Prayer Book of 1549 he could tolerate, but subsequent attacks on the mass, the removal of altars and the Ordinal of 1550 were beyond the pale. After an intense struggle with his conscience he refused conformity, was imprisoned and deprived of his see.[24] Gardiner had supported the royal supremacy because he had seen it as the best method of defending the true faith. When it was used to establish heresy, he realised that he had mistaken his priorities, and at some point between 1550 and 1553, he had returned to the papal allegiance. Similarly placed, Cranmer had nowhere to go. He acknowledged Mary as his lawful monarch, and therefore as supreme head of the church, but both transubstantiation and the papal authority violated his conscience. Worse still, he was soon a condemned traitor. For several weeks after the queen's

---

24 G.R. Redworth, *In Defence of the Church Catholic; a life of Stephen Gardiner.*

accession he had kept a very low profile, only appearing in public to celebrate the late king's funeral with protestant rites on 8 August. However, later in the same month his suffragan, Richard Thornden, began to celebrate mass in Canterbury cathedral, and this led to understandable rumours that the archbishop himself was about to conform to the new regime. Early in September he issued a vehement denial, denouncing the mass as a device of Satan. Summoned before the council on 13 September he refused to retract, or to express any regret for his outspokenness, and was committed to the Tower. Much as the queen may have resented them, his words did not constitute an offence at law, because the mass itself was still illegal, but Cranmer was not so naive as to place any trust in that protection. He sent Margaret and his children secretly into Germany, paid his debts and took leave of his friends before responding to the council's summons. Mary did not wait for the repeal of the Edwardian legislation, let alone the restoration of papal jurisdiction. On 4 November he was indicted of High Treason for his acceptance of King Edward's 'Device' during the summer, and was tried at the Guildhall on 13 November, along with Jane and Guildford Dudley, and Guildford's brothers Henry and Ambrose. Deeply troubled in his conscience, he pleaded not guilty, apparently on the grounds that he had acted in accordance with the late king's personal instructions. If that was the meaning of his gesture, he did not persist, changing his plea before the jury could withdraw, and was duly condemned along with the others. Technically there is no doubt that he was guilty, but these events hit him hard, and a few days later he wrote a humble letter of submission, containing a detailed apology for his conduct, and a plea for mercy on the grounds that others had already been pardoned '. . . which travailed not so much to dissuade the king and his council as I did.'[25] In a sense the queen responded, not because she had any intention of sparing his life, but because she wished to reserve him for a higher condemnation before the authorities which he had most grievously offended - God and the Pope. On 17 December he was allowed the liberty of the Tower garden, and this was a sufficient indication that he was not destined for an early visit to the headsman's block.

As a canonically consecrated archbishop, Cranmer could not be tried by any ecclesiastical court in England which Mary would have been willing to employ, and perhaps because that made the timing of his eventual arraignment uncertain, it was decided to subject him, along with Nicholas Ridley and Hugh Latimer to that form of academic bear baiting called a public disputation. On 8 March the council ordered the removal of all three prisoners to Oxford, where they were lodged in the town gaol, the Bocardo. The council paid them the compliment of commissioning a very high powered team of theologians, including the vice-chancellors of both universities, to dispute against them, but the academic form was a mere pretence. The commissioners were given the power to condemn their adversaries for heresy, should they so decide, although that verdict was not to have the force of a judicial decision. Royal letters of warrant then authorised the mayor of Oxford to hand over his prisoners to the commissioners '. . . so as their erroneous opinions being by the word of God justly and truly con-

---

25 Cranmer, *Miscellaneous writings*, 442. Loades, *Oxford Martyrs*, 119-21.

vinced, the residue of our subjects may be thereby better established in the true catholic faith.'[26] Cranmer was brought before the commissioners in St.Mary's church on 14 April 1554, and presented with a set of articles affirming the catholic doctrine of the mass. His formal rejection of them was then recorded, and he was instructed to submit his replies in writing, returning to dispute on Monday, 16 April. Rather surprisingly, as the authorities later declared it to have been a great triumph for orthodoxy, we do not have any catholic account of the subsequent disputation. From the partisan narrative of Foxe, it appears to have been a disorderly and thoroughly inconclusive performance. Weston, the Prolocutor, made no attempt to keep to the academic form, or even to insist upon the use of the learned language. There was consequently a crossfire of discussion in both latin and English, with no attempt to cast the arguments correctly, or even comprehensibly. The two sides were in any case arguing at cross purposes, from different premises. To Cranmer there could be no separation between substance and accidents - that is between the fundamental nature of the elements and their outward appearance - and consequently the corporeal body of Christ could only be in one place at a time; since the ascension, that was in heaven. Consequently there could be no corporeal presence in the eucharist, which became a physical and philosophical absurdity. To the catholics on the other hand, the substance and the accidents could be separated, and the substance consequently could be divided, so that although the physical presence of the Man Jesus might remain in heaven, there was no intellectual

---

26 John Foxe, *Acts and Monuments of the English Martyrs*, ed. J. Pratt, VI, 531-2.

difficulty in accepting that His substance could be simultaneously in heaven and in a thousand eucharists on earth. The argument as recorded by Foxe was crude, and on Weston's side abusive, but not even Foxe pretends that Cranmer argued effectively.[27] He seems to have been browbeaten and lacking in confidence. Nevertheless he did not give way, and his condemnation was formally pronounced.

Similar treatment was meted out to Ridley and Latimer over the following two days, and they were then returned to separate prisons. If the authorities were hoping to make an abject spectacle of the reforming leaders, they certainly failed, and in fact neither side gained significantly; but Cranmer at least knew where he stood, if he had been in any doubt. Because of its essentially theological nature, this disputation did not strike at the archbishop's achilles heel, and consequently spared him a really serious crisis of conscience. Although he may not have disputed well, be had no doubts about transubstantiation, the sacrifice of the mass, or justification by faith alone. But on the authority of the Christian magistrate he was vulnerable, and this vulnerability was rigorously exploited when he was tried in earnest on 12 September 1555. It had taken some nine months for the papal bureaucracy to go through all the necessary motions, because as *legatus natus*, Cranmer was technically Pole's equal, and could not therefore be tried by a Legatine commission, as Ridley and Latimer were. Only a direct papal commission would suffice, and that required formalities of citation which had to be allowed to take

---

27 *Ibid.*, 468-500.

their course. The papal commissioner was bishop James Brooks of Gloucester, and the sixteen articles with which he confronted Cranmer, and which had probably been drawn up in the office of the Inquisitor General, reveal a more intelligent strategy than any which had hitherto been employed. They avoided controversial issues of theology altogether, and concentrated entirely upon breeches of the canon law which the defendant was bound to admit because they were also positive expressions of his new convictions. He was, for example, charged with matrimony;

> 'Item, that he shameth not openly to glory himself to have had his wife in secret many years . . .'[28]

This approach seems to have taken Cranmer by surprise because, in common with most defendants at the time, he was given no notice of the specific charges. He could only respond somewhat lamely that he had no cause to be ashamed of what he had done. The main substance of the case against him, however, was his rejection of papal authority, a charge which he had no option but to substantiate by refusing to acknowledge the jurisdiction of the court.

Thereafter he was wrong-footed at every turn. Brooks's opening address was nothing but a string of cliches, based upon the inevitable assumption that the church could only be defined by acceptance of the Roman jurisdiction, and that the deviant was condemned by the mere

---

28 Foxe, VIII, 58.

fact of deviation. Technically Brooks was the judge, and Martin and Story, the royal proctors, were the accusers, but in fact, as Cranmer quite rightly protested later, Brooks was both advocate and judge because the papacy was actually a party to the case. Charged with having broken his original oath to the Pope, the archbishop admitted the fact, but pointed out that there were few in authority in the English church who could escape the same charge, certainly not Brooks himself, who had accepted the royal supremacy in the time of King Henry. The king and queen also, he claimed, had taken oaths to uphold the laws of England, and were consequently perjured by having submitted to a foreign jurisdiction.

> 'By the scripture the king is chief, and no foreign person in his realm above him. There is no subject but to a king. I am a subject, I owe my fidelity to the Crown . . . you at the beginning of your oration declared by the sword and the keys, attributing the keys to the Pope and the sword to the king. But I say the king has both . . .'[29]

Cranmer had no difficulty in rehearsing his familiar arguments in favour of the royal jurisdiction, but their effect was entirely destroyed when the king himself refused to accept them. It was the greatest grief he had ever known, he protested, to be accused by his lawful sovereigns in their own realm, before a foreign power. They were apostates, and traitors to their own estate, but unfortunately that did not impair their lawful authority.

---

29 *Ibid.*, 51.

John Story exploited his advantage ruthlessly. If Cranmer was the good subject which he professed to be, why did he not obey the queen's explicit orders? It was no good pleading the laws of England as though they were something immutable, when he knew perfectly well that they could be changed every year.

> '. . . the same laws, being put away by a parliament, are now received again by a parliament, and have as full authority now as they had then; and they will now that ye answer to the Pope's holiness; therefore by the laws of this realm ye are bound to answer him.'[30]

Having exposed the fragility of the royal supremacy in practice, the proctors then proceeded, to their own satisfaction, to demonstrate its absurdity in theory. If the Pope is not Head of the Church, demanded Martin, then who is? 'Christ', responded Cranmer, predictably. In that case, who is Christ's vicar on earth? 'Nobody' replied the archbishop, meaning that in his eyes there was no single Vicar of Christ for the whole church. In that case '. . . why told you not King Henry this when you made him Supreme Head? . . . This is treason against his own person as you then made him.' Was Nero supreme head of the church when he lawfully held the Imperial dignity? Yes, replied Cranmer, 'in worldly respect of the temporal bodies of men'. Martin ignored the qualification, and pressed his point home triumphantly:

---

30 *Ibid.*, 54.

> 'Then he that beheaded the heads of the church, and crucified the apostles, was Head of Christ's church; and he that was never member of the church is head of the church by your new found understanding of God's word . . .'[31]

It was, from the protestant point of view, a disastrous performance. Cranmer seems to have been consistently unable to find the right words to put his case in a valid or persuasive form, and to have made little or no use of the solid arguments which abound in his published works. Advancing years and intimidating circumstances may partly account for this, but the main reason seems to have been his genuine dilemma of conscience. Whatever Martin or Brooks might allege, his adherence to the Royal Supremacy had always been a matter of principle. This had led him into some devious paths, as over his oath to the pope or the Boleyn marriage, but in his own eyes his duty to the king had absolved him. Why, therefore, should his duty to the queen not now absolve him from the sins of celebrating mass or submitting to the pope? Might not God once again be speaking through the royal will? Foxe, recording his trial later, was clearly puzzled by his unconvincing performance, and tried to blame it upon the partisan notary who had recorded the exchanges.[32] Others noticed the same signs. The Spanish friar, Petro de Soto, scenting a recantation, began to visit him; '. . . if he can be brought to repent, the church will derive no little benefit from the salvation of a single soul.' De Soto overplayed his hand by forcing the arch-

---

31 Loades, *Oxford Martyrs*, 201.

32 Foxe, VIII, 58.

bishop to witness the executions of his friends Nicholas Ridley and Hugh Latimer, who had been tried a few days after him. Their steadfastness strengthened him, and on 23 October the Spaniard expressed despair of achieving his objective.[33] However, by the beginning of 1556 Cranmer was weakening again. Because he had been duly consecrated, it took almost as long to dispose of him as it had to bring him to trial, and this allowed time for many fluctuations in his resolution. He wrote a long justification of his position to the queen, and considered appealing to a General Council. At the beginning of January 1556 Cranmer was informed that the formal process of his condemnation had been completed in Rome, and that he had been 'relaxed' to the secular arm. At the same time he was placed in close confinement, and began to be visited by another Spanish friar, Juan de Villagarcia. About the middle of January he signed his first recantation, the break predictably coming at his weakest point;

> 'Forasmuch as the King and Queen's majesties, by consent of their parliament, have received the Pope's authority within this realm, I am content to submit myself to their laws herein, and to take the pope for the chief head of the church of England, so far as God's laws and the laws and customs of this realm will permit.'[34]

This was far too equivocal to satisfy Villagarcia, or any-

---

33 De Soto to Monsignor Priuli; *Calendar of State Papers, Venetian*, ed. Rawdon et al., VI, 256.

34 Cranmer, *Miscellaneous writings*, App. xliii.

one else, but having once broken down, he was persuaded to sign a much more explicit submission a few days later, placing himself at the mercy of the Pope, the King and the Queen.

Although news of this collapse must have been conveyed to Pole within a few days, there was at first no reaction at all, either from Westminster or Lambeth. In all probability it was a cause of embarrassment rather than satisfaction. Mary had deliberately reserved Cranmer for the fire, when she could easily have executed him for treason. She had no intention of allowing the man whom she chiefly blamed for the woes of England and the traumas of her own life to go unpunished; but executing a heretic who had recanted and not relapsed was contrary to both law and custom. Pole equally had a personal mission of vengeance to pursue. In November 1555, after the trial, he had written to Cranmer in a cold fury

> 'This your charity you now show to your country, which as I said hitherto, is a very vengeance of God towards you . . . as though you had never knowledge what had been done in the realm before your time, nor yet what is the state of the realm at this present . . . but if (ignorance) do not excuse you, then malice doth condemn you; which is the very cause to bring you to ignorance inexcusable, both in this point of the authority of the pope, as in the doctrine of the sacrament, wherein it is no less monstrous.'[35]

35 *Ibid.*, App. xliv.

This was hardly the letter of a confessor to a penitent, and it seems that the Cardinal held him personally responsible for the disaster which had overtaken his own family between 1538 and 1541. Like the queen, he had no intention of relenting, and the preparations for Cranmer's execution continued. On 14 February he was publicly degraded in Christ Church by bishops Thirlby and Bonner, a protracted and distasteful ritual designed to humiliate the victim. The only official comment made upon his recantation was that it was insincere, with the clear implication that it would be ignored. On 24 February a writ *de heretico comburendo* was issued. Meanwhile the Spanish friars in Oxford, with innocent zeal and fearing the relapse of their penitent, continued to press him for a fuller and more explicit confession of all his heretical errors, not just those relating to the papal authority. This they obtained on 26 February, and at the beginning of March it was published in London by the printers Rydall and Copland.[36] By 12 March the news was public property, and it was believed that Cranmer would be paraded for a great ceremony of recantation.

The queen seems to have been distinctly annoyed by this development. On 13 March the printers were summoned before the council, and their work suppressed without any official reason being given. The news, however, could not be suppressed, and the decision seems to have been taken to proceed on the grounds that nothing said by such a man, however explicit, was worthy of credence. Foxe's verdict was hardly impartial, but in this case was not very far from the truth;

---

36 *All the submyssyons and recantations of T. Cranmer. Oxford Martyrs*, 229-30.

'The Queen, having now gotten a time to revenge her old grief, received his recantation
very gladly, but of her purpose to put him to
death she would nothing relent . . .'[37]

On 18 March Crammer signed his sixth and final confession, but it was by then clear to him that there was no
chance of saving his life, and he began to prepare a
humble and submissive speech to deliver at the stake, in
accordance with the conventional wisdom of 'making a
good end'. However, even as he completed this task,
the old man's mind began to change again. He was
sixty seven years old, and in an extremity beyond the
fear of death. The royal supremacy, after all, was a
means to an end, and not an end in itself. The end was
the establishment of a true church, and only a few months
before he had been quite clear as to what the nature of
that church must be. Perhaps there were greater sins
than disobedience to a lawful monarch. It was not Queen
Mary to whom he would have to render account now,
nor Henry VIII, but God. He sat down and wrote an
alternative ending to his submissive speech, in which his
penitence became redirected to his own weakness, and to
the friends and colleagues whose sacrifices he had be-
littled by his surrender. When he went from Bocardo to
St. Mary's church on the morning of 21 March, we do
not know whether he had already made up his mind to
cheat the expectations of his persecutors, or whether he
was still in a state of knife-edge indecision. He seems to
have reassured the bystanders of the genuineness of his
submission, and even to have signed extra copies of his

37 Foxe, VIII, 83.

recantation.

It was perhaps only after Dr. Cole, the Provost of Eton, had described his coming death as a just recompense for the execution of John Fisher, that Cranmer finally made up his mind. Not only was the government proposing to execute an ostensibly penitent sinner, it was also justifying its action in terms of revenge. If the victim was looking for a sign, he might well have found it in this unworthy oration, and when he came to offer his own final testimony, his conscience was at peace.

> 'And now I come to the great thing which so much troubleth my conscience . . . and that is the setting abroad of a writing contrary to the truth; which I now here renounce and refuse . . . And as for the Pope, I refuse him as Christ's enemy and antichrist with his false doctrine. And as for the sacrament, I believe as I have taught in my book against the bishop of Winchester . . .'[38]

A Godly magistrate might command the total obedience of a Christian man. Edward had been such a prince, and so in his own way had Henry. But Philip and Mary were not Godly magistrates, and in the last analysis the allegiance which they could command must be limited and conditional. The impact of this speech was tremendous; it was a *coup de theatre*, and the news of it spread like wildfire. Protestants until recently dismayed by the collapse of such a long respected leader, took fresh heart,

---

38 *Ibid.*, 88. British Library MS Cotton Titus A xxiv, f.87.

and told themselves that God had strengthened him at the last, having allowed his weakness as a warning against spiritual pride. At the same time, of course, he had rescued the queen and the cardinal from their embarrassment. On 24 March Giovanni Michieli, the Venetian ambassador, reported to his government;

> 'On Saturday last, the 21, Cranmer, late archbishop of Canterbury was burned, having fully verified the opinion formed of him by the Queen, that he had feigned recantation thinking to save his life, and not that he had received any good inspiration, so she considered him unworthy of pardon . . .'[39]

It was a temporary relief, for Cranmer was a great deal more potent dead than alive, and with his restraining influence removed, some of the hotter sort of protestants began to move decisively towards resistance theory. Within two years Christopher Goodman and John Knox were preaching the violent overthrow of antichrist.[40]

VI

Martyrdom

Thomas Cranmer therefore died as a martyr, not for the

---

39 *Calendar of State Papers, Venetian*, VI, 434.

40 Christopher Goodman, *How superior powers ought to be obeyed* (Geneva, 1558); John Knox, *The Apellation of John Knox* (Geneva, 1558).

royal supremacy but for protestant doctrine, and the legacy which he bequeathed to the English church was both erastian and evangelical. It was a more potent legacy than that of Goodman and Knox, because when protestantism returned to England with Elizabeth, it was as an establishment upon the Edwardian model. In 1559 the new queen set out to play the part of a Godly Magistrate, and thus to eliminate the conditional element in the allegiance of her protestant subjects. The Elizabethan settlement pleased few, but it was acceptable to most, because the tradition which it represented was the tradition which had been forged by Henry and Cranmer between 1534 and 1547. The English church was an aspect of the autonomous nation, ruled by the same head and governor. It was not, in fact, a very logical settlement, because the tension between royal and scriptural authority, which had so plagued Cranmer in his last days, was never far beneath the surface. It emerged to some extent in late sixteenth century puritanism, and much more forcibly in the sectarianism of the 1640s. However, it was a practical settlement. Given reasonable commonsense, it worked precisely because it was not exclusively dependant upon doctrinal commitment. Nevertheless it was capable of sophisticated intellectual justification, as Richard Hooker was to demonstrate. Elizabeth chose it because it was a means to make the church serve the purposes of her government, and because pluralism was not an option in the English context. It was available to her because Thomas Cranmer had managed to run an erastian church and to die for a protestant one. Of course, he had a little help from his friends - notably Nicholas Ridley during his lifetime and John Foxe after his death - but it was his unique achievement to give spiritual credibility to what could so easily have been no more than a piece of sordid opportunism. He was not a saint, or a hero, and was a martyr very much against his will, but he was a man of faith and integrity. A generation after his death it could be said

> 'Religion and policy are, through God's singular blessing, preserved together in life as with one spirit; he that doth take away the life of the one doth procure the death of the other . . .'[41]

and that extraordinarily durable amalgam of protestant nationalism was one of the most significant legacies of the period to subsequent English history. If there was one thing which was to prove more central to English culture than Cranmer's magnificent liturgical prose, it was that sense of a special providence which traced the historiography of the divine purpose from John Wycliffe to the imperial drama of the nineteenth century. And in that process, Thomas Cranmer was both the crucial link and the creative statesman.

---

41 William Charke, *Answer to a Seditious Pamphlet* (1580), sig. C 1.

Select bibliography

Sources:
J.G. Nichols (ed.) *Narratives of the Days of the Reformation* (Camden Society, 1859)

The Works of Thomas Cranmer, ed. J. E. Cox (Parker Society, 1844, 1846)

John Foxe, *The Acts and Monuments of these latter and perilous days*, ed. G. Townsend and S.R. Cattley (1837-1841)

E. Surtz and V. Murphy (eds.) *The Divorce Tracts of Henry VIII* (Angers, 1987)

G. Bedouelle and P. Le Gal (eds.) *Le 'Divorce' du Roi Henry VIII* (Geneva, 1987)

Secondary works:
P. Brooks, *Thomas Cranmer's Doctrine of the Eucharist* (1965)

G.W. Bromiley, *Thomas Cranmer, archbishop and martyr* (1955)

G.W. Bromiley, *Thomas Cranmer, theologian* (1956)

W.A. Clebsch, *England's earliest protestants* (Westport, Connecticut, 1964)

A.G. Dickens, *The English Reformation* (2nd ed., 1989)

C.W. Dugmore, *The mass and the English reformers* (1958)

J. Guy, *Tudor England* (Oxford, 1988)

P. Hughes, *The Reformation in England* (1950-1954)

D.M. Loades, *The Oxford Martyrs* (1970)

G. Nicholson, 'The Act of Appeals and the English Reformation', in C. Cross, D. Loades and J. Scarisbrick (eds.) *Law and Government under the Tudors* (Cambridge, 1988)

E.C. Ratcliff, 'The Liturgical works of Archbishop Cranmer', in *Journal of Ecclesiastical History*, VII, 1956, 189-203

Jasper Ridley, *Thomas Cranmer* (1962)

J.J. Scarisbrick, *Henry VIII* (1968)

J. Strype, *Ecclesiastical Memorials* (1721)

S. Brigden, *The Reformation in London during the reign of Henry VIII* (1989)

G.R. Redworth, *In Defence of the Church Catholic; a life of Stephen Gardiner* (1990)

Diarmid McCulloch is currently working on a new biography of Cranmer

Bibliography of David Loades

1960
'The authorship and publication of ...(*STC* 3480)', *Transactions of the Cambridge Bibliographical Society*, III, ii, 1960, 1955-60

1962
'The Essex Inquisitions of 1556', *Bulletin of the Institute of Historical Research*, XXXV, 1962, 87-97

1964
'The Press under the early Tudors', *Transactions of the Cambridge Bibliographical Society*, IV, i, 1964, 29-50

1965
'The enforcement of reaction, 1553-1558', *Journal of Ecclesiastical History*, XVI, i 1965, 54-66
Two Tudor Conspiracies (C.U.P. 1965)

1967
'The Collegiate Churches of County Durham at the time of the Dissolution', *Studies in Church History*, IV, 1967, 65-75

1968
The Papers of George Wyatt, (Editor D.M.L.) Camden Society, Fourth Series, 5

1970
The Oxford Martyrs (Batsford 1970)
'The last years of Cuthbert Tunstall, 1547-1559'. *Durham University Journal* LXVI, 1973, 10-22

1974

'The theory and practice of censorship in sixteenth century England', *Transactions of the Royal Historical Society*', Fifth Series, XXIV, 1974, 141-50

Politics and the Nation, 1450-1660, (1974, 4th edn. Fontana 1992)

1975

'England and Wales, 1955-70' *Bibliography of the Reform, 450-1648* (Edited by D.M.L. and Derek Baker), Blackwell, 1975, 1-180

1979

'The Royal Supremacy: a note in discussion,' *The Urban Classes, the Nobility and the Reformation*, German Historical Institute, 1979, 128-30

The Reign of Mary Tudor, Benn, 1979 (2nd Edn. Longmans, 1991)

1980

'The Netherlands and the Anglo-Papal Reconciliation of 1554', *Nederlands Archief voor Kercheschiedenis*, LX 1980, 39-55

'Anabaptism and English Sectarianism in the mid-Sixteenth century', *Studies in Church History*, subsidia 2, 1980, 59-70

1981

(With C.A. Haigh) 'The fortunes of the shrine of St Mary of Caversham', *Oxoniensia*, XLVI, 1981, 62-72.

1982

'Elisabeth Ire, la reine de la propagande politique'. *L'his-*

toire, XLIII, 1982, 48-58

'The origins of English Protestant Nationalism', *Studies in Church History*, XVIII, 1982, 297-307

'Relations between the Anglican and Roman Catholic Churches in the Sixteenth and Seventeenth Centuries', *Rome and the Anglicans*, ed. Wolfgang Haase, 1982, 1-53

Maria Tudor (Calwey, Munich, 1982)

1984

The End of Strife, (Ed. D.M.L.) (Durham C.I.H.E.C. Colloquium, 1981) T. and T. Clark, 1984.

1985

'Warfare and International Relations, 1450-1625' (ed. C.A. Haigh), *The Cambridge Historical Encyclopedia of Great Britain and Ireland*, 1985, 171-175

1986

The Tudor Court (Batsford, 1986)

1987

'Introduction' and 'The dissolution of the Diocese of Durham, 1553-4', (ed. D. Marcombe), *The Last Principality*, 1987, 1-6, 101-116

(with J.D. Alsop) 'William Paulet, First Marquis of Winchester; a question of age', *Sixteenth Century Journal*, XVIII, 1987, 333-43

'The bishops of the restored catholic church under Queen Mary', *Miscellanea Historiae Ecclesiastica*, VIII, 1987, 343-55

1988

'Philip II and the Government of England', *Law and Government under the Tudors* (Eds. D.M.L. with M.C. Cross and J.J. Scarisbrick), C.U.P. 1988.
'The Boy King and Bloody Mary', *Armada 400*, 1988
'Gairdner, James', and 'Lingard, John', *Blackwell's Dictionary of Historians*, (ed. J. Cannon,) 1988
'Illicit Presses and Clandestine Printing in England, 1520-90', *Too Mighty to be Free; censorship and the Press in Britain and the Netherlands*, ed. A. Duke, 1988, 1-27

1989

Mary Tudor, a life (Blackwell, 1989, pbk 1992)
'The Reign of Mary Tudor: Historiography and Research', *Albion*, XXI, iv, 1989, 547-58

1990

'Le Livre et la Réforme anglaise avant 1558', *La Réforme el le livre; L'Europe de L'imprimé* (1517-v.1570), ed. M Gilmont, 1990, 269-300
The Tudor Court, Historical Association, 1990
Chronicles of the Tudor Kings, (Edited by D.M.L.) Garamond, 1990
Faith and Identity (Studies in church History, subsidia 6) (Ed. with Katherine Walsh) Blackwell, 1990

1991

Politics, Censorship and the English Reformation (Pinter, 1991)
'The Keeping of the Seas; the King's Ships, 1413-1480', *Medieval History* Vol.I, i, 1991
'The Renaissance Court: England, Italy and Burgundy', *Medieval History* Vol.I, iii, 1991

The Reign of Mary Tudor (see 1979)

In press

'The piety of the restored Catholic church under Queen Mary', *Humanism and Reform in Britain and the Continent*, *essays presented to Professor J.K. Cameron*, (ed. J. Kirk) (Studies in Church History, subsidia 7, 1991)
'Select document, 1485-1608': Navy Record Society Centenary Volume Sec.2, for the Navy Record Society
The Mid-Tudor Crisis (Macmillan)
Revolution in Religion: the English Reformation (University of Wales Press)
A History of the Navy in the Sixteenth Century (Gower Press)

In progress

John Dudley, Duke of Northumberland: a political biography (O.U.P.)

Re-issues of   Two Tudor Conspiracies
                The Oxford Martyrs
                The Tudor Court

Headstart History is currently negotiating rights with C.U.P. and Batsford.